GRENOBLE TRAVEL GUIDE 2024-2025

Discover the City's Charm, Cultural Attractions, and Mountain Adventures

ALEXANDER PAUL

Copyright© 2024 ALEXANDER PAUL

All rights reserved.
No part of this book may be reproduced, stored in a retrieval system, or transmitted in any form or by any means, electronic, mechanical, photocopying, recording, or otherwise, without the prior written permission of the publisher. Unauthorized reproduction of this book, or parts thereof, is prohibited by law and may result in legal action.

3

Table of Contents

Chapter 1: Welcome to Grenoble   15
   Discovering Grenoble   16
   History and Culture   17
   What Makes Grenoble Special Today   18

Chapter 2: Traveling to Grenoble   21
   By Air   22
   By Train   22
   By Car   23
   By Bus   24
   Travel Tips   25

Chapter 3: Navigating Grenoble   27
   Public Transportation   28
   Trams   28
   Buses   29
   Cycling and Walking   29
   Cycling   30
   Walking   30
   Car Rentals and Taxis   31
   Car Rentals   31
   Taxis   31
   Accessibility in Grenoble   32

Chapter 4: Accommodation in Grenoble   34
   Luxury Hotels   34
      Le Grand Hôtel Grenoble Centre   34
      Hôtel Mercure Grenoble Centre Alpotel   35
      Park Hôtel Grenoble - MGallery   36

Mid-Range Hotels	37
Ibis Styles Grenoble Centre Gare	37
Hôtel Europole	38
Okko Hotels Grenoble Jardin Hoche	38
Budget-Friendly Options	38
Résidhotel Grenette	39
Hôtel Alizé	39
B&B Hôtel Grenoble Centre Alpexpo	39
Unique and Boutique Stays	40
Maison Barbillon Grenoble	40
Hôtel d'Angleterre	40
Le Hüb by Privilodges	41
Chapter 5: Must-See Sights	**42**
Bastille Fort	42
History and Significance	42
Visiting the Fort	43
Grenoble Museum (Musée de Grenoble)	43
Collection Highlights	44
Visiting Information	44
Musée Dauphinois	45
Visiting Information	46
Paul Mistral Park	46
Grenoble-Bastille Cable Car	48
The Experience	48
Archaeological Museum (Musée Archéologique Grenoble Saint-Laurent)	49
Chapter 6 Exploring Grenoble's Quarters	**51**
City Center	52
Quartier Saint-Laurent	53

Île Verte	54
Europole	55
Presqu'île	56
Chapter 7: Cultural Experiences	**58**
Art, Music, and Theater	58
Art Galleries	59
Musée de Grenoble	59
Magasin - Centre National d'Art Contemporain	59
Galerie Vent des Cimes	60
Performing Arts Venues	60
La MC2: Maison de la Culture	60
Théâtre de Grenoble	61
L'Ampérage	61
Music Festivals	61
Festival de Musique de Chambre	61
Cabaret Frappé	62
Les Détours de Babel	62
Annual Events	63
Fête des Lumières	63
Festival du Film Court en Plein Air	63
Marché de Noël	63
Chapter 8: Embracing Nature	**66**
Hiking Trails	67
Chartreuse Mountains	67
Vercors Regional Natural Park	67
Belledonne Range	68
Cycling Routes	68
La Véloroute du Val de Drôme	68
Grenoble to Lake Geneva	69

Bike Paths in Grenoble	69
Skiing and Snowboarding	69
Alpe d'Huez	70
Les Deux Alpes	70
Chamrousse	70
Parks and Gardens	71
Jardin de Ville	71
Parc Paul Mistral	71
Water Sports	71
Isère River	72
Lac de Monteynard	72
Chapter 9: Retail Therapy	**73**
Local Markets	74
Marché des Halles Sainte-Claire	74
Marché de l'Estacade	75
Marché de Bérivière	75
Shopping Centers	75
Grand'Place	75
Carrefour Grenoble Cité	76
Centre Commercial La Tronche	76
Boutiques and Specialty Shops	77
L'Atelier de la Mode	77
Le Comptoir de la Malle	77
Maison du Chocolat	78
Souvenirs and Local Crafts	78
Les Artisans du Monde	78
Boutique du Musée de Grenoble	78
La Boutique de la Maison de la Culture	79
Chapter 10: Gastronomic Delights	**80**

Traditional Alpine Dishes	81
Fondue Savoyarde	81
Raclette	82
Tartiflette	82
Fine Dining Restaurants	82
Le Fantin Latour	83
Le Gavroche	83
Le Bistrot de l'Artisan	83
Bistros and Cafés	84
Café de l'Industrie	84
Le Comptoir du Marché	84
La Brasserie de la Gare	85
Vegetarian and Vegan Options	85
L'Artichaut	85
Le Vieux Fusil	86
Greenhouse Café	86
Local Wineries and Breweries	86
Domaine de la Côte	87
Brasserie du Mont Blanc	87
Vignoble de Grenoble	87
Chapter 11: Evening Adventures	**89**
Bars and Pubs	90
Le Bar du Bureau	90
La Maison de la Biere	90
Le Comptoir des Alpes	91
Nightclubs	91
Le Club 360	91
La Belle Époque	92
Le Fizz	92

Live Music Venues	93
La Belle Electrique	93
Le 38 Riv' Café	93
L'Antre-Peaux	94
Cultural Nights	94
Théâtre de Grenoble	94
Le Magasin – Centre National d'Art Contemporain	95
Grenoble International Film Festival	95
Chapter 12: Exploring Beyond Grenoble	**97**
Chartreuse Mountains	98
La Grande Chartreuse Monastery	98
Hiking Trails	98
Villages and Local Cuisine	99
Vercors Regional Natural Park	99
Gorges de la Bourne	100
Villard-de-Lans	100
Caving and Climbing	100
Lyon	101
Vieux Lyon	101
Lyon's Culinary Scene	101
Annecy	102
Lake Annecy	102
Annecy's Old Town	102
Chambéry	103
Château de Chambéry	103
Chambéry's Old Town	103
Chapter 13 Fun for All Ages	**105**
Family-Friendly Museums	105

Grenoble Museum	105
Musée Dauphinois	105
La Casemate	106
Parks and Playgrounds	106
Paul Mistral Park	106
Jardin de Ville	107
Parc de la Poya	107
Interactive Exhibits	108
Le Magasin – Centre National d'Art Contemporain	108
The Natural History Museum of Grenoble	108
Kid-Friendly Restaurants	108
La Table de l'Ours	109
Le Café des Arts	109
La Crêperie des Alpes	109
Chapter 14: Visitor Essentials	**111**
Tourist Information Centers	111
Grenoble Tourist Office	111
Grenoble-Alpes Métropole Tourist Office	112
Emergency Contacts	112
Emergency Services	112
Medical Services	112
Local Customs and Etiquette	113
Greetings and Communication	113
Dining Etiquette	113
Currency and Banking	113
Currency	114
Banking Services	114
Currency Exchange	114

Language Tips	114
Basic French Phrases	114
Pronunciation Tips	115
Chapter 15: Making the Most of Your Visit	**116**
Best Times to Visit	116
Spring (March to May)	116
Summer (June to August)	116
Autumn (September to November)	117
Winter (December to February)	117
Safety Tips	117
General Safety	117
Travel Safety	117
Budgeting for Your Trip	118
Accommodation Costs	118
Dining Costs	118
Transportation Costs	119
Eco-Friendly Travel Practices	119
Sustainable Transportation	119
Responsible Tourism	119
Conservation Efforts	120
Chapter 16: Grenoble for Business	**121**
Conference Venues	121
WTC Grenoble (World Trade Center Grenoble)	121
Palais des Congrès de Grenoble	122
La Caserne de Bonne	122
Business Services	122
Co-Working Spaces	122
Business Centers	123
Networking Spots	124

Business Lunch Spots	124
Networking Events and Conferences	125
Tips for Business Travelers	125
Communication	125
Time Management	125
Local Etiquette	126
Accommodation	126

Chapter 1: Welcome to Grenoble

Discovering Grenoble

Nestled in the heart of the French Alps, Grenoble is a city that marries the best of nature and urban living. Known as the "Capital of the Alps," Grenoble is surrounded by majestic mountain ranges, offering breathtaking views and a plethora of outdoor activities year-round. This dynamic city is a haven for outdoor enthusiasts, history buffs, and culture seekers alike.

Grenoble's unique geography makes it an ideal destination for those who love nature. Whether you're hiking through verdant trails in the summer or skiing down powdery slopes in the winter, the surrounding mountains provide endless opportunities for adventure. The city itself is equally inviting, with a vibrant urban landscape characterized by a mix of modern architecture and historic charm.

History and Culture

Grenoble's history dates back over two millennia. Originally a Gallic settlement, it became a significant Roman city known as Cularo. Over the centuries, Grenoble evolved, becoming a crucial hub during the Middle Ages and later, a center of the French Revolution. Each era left its mark, contributing to the city's rich tapestry of historical and cultural landmarks.

The Bastille, a fortress perched on the mountainside overlooking the city, is a testament to Grenoble's strategic importance. Constructed in the 19th century, it now serves as a popular tourist attraction, accessible via a scenic cable car ride that offers panoramic views of the city and surrounding Alps.

Grenoble is also known for its academic and scientific contributions. Home to several prestigious universities and research institutions, including the renowned Université Grenoble Alpes, the city has a vibrant student population and a reputation for innovation. The CEA Grenoble, a major scientific research center, underscores the city's role as a leader in technology and research.

The cultural fabric of Grenoble is enriched by its museums and art galleries. The Musée de Grenoble, one of France's premier art museums, houses an impressive collection of artwork spanning centuries. From classical masterpieces to contemporary works, the museum offers a journey through the evolution of art. The Musée Dauphinois provides insights into the regional heritage, showcasing exhibits on the history and culture of the Dauphiné region.

What Makes Grenoble Special Today

Grenoble's allure today is a blend of its natural beauty, historical depth, and vibrant modernity. The city is a bustling center for commerce and innovation, with a thriving tech industry that has earned it the nickname "Silicon Valley of the Alps." Major tech companies and startups alike find a home here, fostering an environment of creativity and forward-thinking.

Yet, despite its modern advancements, Grenoble retains a strong connection to its roots. The city's architecture reflects this duality, with cutting-edge buildings standing alongside well-preserved historical sites. Walking through Grenoble's streets, one can admire the elegant Place Grenette, a central square lined with charming cafés and shops, or explore the medieval streets of the old town, where each corner reveals a piece of the city's storied past.

The local cuisine is another highlight. Grenoble is famous for its walnuts, a key ingredient in many local dishes and desserts. The surrounding region, rich in agricultural bounty, contributes fresh produce to the city's markets, where you can sample cheeses, meats, and other delicacies unique to the area. Dining in Grenoble is a delight, with a range of options from traditional bistros to gourmet restaurants.

Grenoble's commitment to sustainability is evident in its policies and urban planning. The city has extensive cycling paths, efficient public transportation, and numerous green spaces, reflecting a dedication to environmentally-friendly living. This focus on sustainability not only enhances the quality of life for residents but also makes Grenoble an appealing destination for eco-conscious travelers.

Festivals and events are integral to Grenoble's cultural life. The city hosts numerous festivals throughout the year, celebrating everything from music and cinema to science and innovation. The annual Grenoble Jazz Festival, for instance, attracts world-class musicians and jazz enthusiasts from around the globe. Such events foster a sense of community and highlight the city's cultural vibrancy.

Sports are another pillar of Grenoble's identity. The city has a strong sporting tradition, having hosted the 1968 Winter

Olympics. Today, Grenoble continues to be a hub for winter sports, with easy access to some of the best ski resorts in the Alps. In the summer, the city transforms into a base for hiking, mountain biking, and rock climbing, making it a year-round playground for outdoor enthusiasts.

Grenoble's blend of natural splendor, historical richness, and modern innovation makes it a truly unique destination. Whether you're exploring its ancient streets, indulging in local cuisine, or embarking on an alpine adventure, Grenoble offers a diverse array of experiences that captivate and inspire. Welcome to Grenoble, where every visit is an opportunity to discover something extraordinary.

Chapter 2: Traveling to Grenoble

By Air

Grenoble is well-connected to major European cities by air, making it an accessible destination for international travelers. The primary gateway is Grenoble Alpes-Isère Airport (GNB), located approximately 45 kilometers northwest of the city center. This airport handles seasonal flights from various European destinations, particularly during the winter months when ski tourism peaks.

For more frequent flight options, travelers often use Lyon-Saint Exupéry Airport (LYS), situated about 100 kilometers from Grenoble. Lyon's airport is a major international hub, offering a wider range of flights from across the globe. From Lyon-Saint Exupéry, you can reach Grenoble by a direct shuttle bus, which takes around 1.5 hours, or by train, with connections available via the TGV (high-speed train).

Additionally, Geneva Airport (GVA) in Switzerland is another viable option, especially for those traveling from international destinations outside Europe. Geneva is about 150 kilometers from Grenoble and offers numerous direct flights from various continents. Direct buses and shuttle services connect Geneva Airport to Grenoble, making it a convenient choice despite the longer distance.

By Train

Grenoble's central location in southeastern France makes it a key rail hub, well-served by both high-speed TGV trains and regional TER services. The city's main railway station, Gare de Grenoble, is located in the heart of the city, offering easy access to downtown and surrounding areas.

From Paris, the TGV takes approximately three hours to reach Grenoble, making it an efficient option for travelers from the French capital. Trains from other major cities like Lyon, Marseille, and Lille also provide direct connections, facilitating seamless travel across the country. For instance, the journey from Lyon to Grenoble takes about 1.5 hours by train.

Regional TER trains connect Grenoble with nearby cities and towns, including Chambéry, Annecy, and Valence. These services are particularly useful for exploring the Rhône-Alpes region and accessing smaller destinations not served by the TGV.

Booking train tickets in advance is recommended, especially during peak travel seasons. The French national railway company, SNCF, offers various fare options and discounts, including passes for frequent travelers and tourists.

By Car

Traveling to Grenoble by car offers the flexibility to explore the surrounding regions at your own pace. The city is well-connected by a network of highways, making it easily accessible from various parts of France and neighboring countries.

From Lyon, take the A43 motorway towards Chambéry, then merge onto the A41 towards Grenoble. The drive typically takes around 1.5 hours, depending on traffic. If you're coming from Geneva, follow the A41 southbound for approximately two hours.

Driving from Paris involves a longer journey of about 5.5 hours. Take the A6 motorway towards Lyon, then switch to the A43 and A41 as you approach Grenoble. This scenic route offers views of the French countryside and the Alps as you near your destination.

Grenoble's city center can be navigated by car, but parking can be challenging. It's advisable to use one of the numerous public parking garages and rely on public transportation or walking to explore the central areas. Be mindful of local traffic regulations and tolls on French highways, which can add to travel costs.

By Bus

Long-distance buses are a cost-effective way to travel to Grenoble, with several companies offering routes from major French and European cities. FlixBus, Ouibus, and Eurolines are among the popular providers, offering comfortable and affordable services.

Buses from Paris to Grenoble typically take around 8-10 hours, with overnight options available for those who prefer to travel while sleeping. From Lyon, the bus journey is shorter, taking approximately 1.5 to 2 hours.

Grenoble's main bus station, Gare Routière, is conveniently located next to the train station, providing easy transfers between different modes of transport. From here, local buses and trams can take you to your accommodation or other parts of the city.

Travel Tips

1. Advance Planning: Book your travel tickets in advance, especially during peak seasons like winter and summer holidays. This ensures better availability and often, lower prices.

2. Multi-Mode Travel: Consider combining different modes of transport for a seamless journey. For instance, flying into Lyon or Geneva and then taking a train or bus to Grenoble can be both time-efficient and cost-effective.

3. Weather Considerations: Grenoble's alpine location means that weather can be unpredictable. Check the forecast before traveling, especially if you're driving, as mountain roads can be challenging in winter conditions.

4. Local Transport: Once in Grenoble, make use of the efficient public transportation system. The city's tram and bus network is extensive and convenient for getting around without a car.

5. Eco-Friendly Travel: Grenoble is committed to sustainability, and eco-conscious travelers will find numerous green travel options. Use public transportation, rent bicycles, or simply explore on foot to reduce your carbon footprint.

6. Connectivity: Grenoble offers excellent connectivity, but having a local SIM card or portable Wi-Fi device can be useful for navigating, especially if you plan to explore remote areas or use digital maps extensively.

7. Language: While many people in Grenoble speak English, learning a few basic French phrases can enhance your travel experience and help you navigate more easily.

Traveling to Grenoble is a straightforward and enjoyable experience, with multiple options to suit different preferences and budgets. Whether you arrive by air, train, car, or bus, the journey sets the stage for the adventures that await in this vibrant alpine city.

Chapter 3: Navigating Grenoble

Public Transportation

Grenoble boasts a well-developed and efficient public transportation system that makes getting around the city easy and convenient. The primary modes of public transport are trams and buses, operated by the regional transport authority, Société d'Économie Mixte des Transports Publics de l'Agglomération Grenobloise (TAG).

Trams

The tram network is the backbone of Grenoble's public transport system. With five lines (A, B, C, D, and E), the trams cover a substantial portion of the city and its suburbs. The trams are modern, frequent, and reliable, making them a popular choice for both locals and tourists.

- **Line A** runs from Fontaine-La Poya to Échirolles Denis Papin, passing through key areas like the city center and the main train station, Gare de Grenoble.
- **Line B** connects the northern suburb of Presqu'île to Gières Plaine des Sports, serving important stops such as the University of Grenoble.
- **Line C** travels between Seyssins Le Prisme and Saint-Martin-d'Hères Condillac Universités, providing access to various residential and commercial areas.
- **Line D** links Saint-Martin-le-Vinoux Hôtel de Ville to the southern suburb of Pont-de-Claix L'Étoile.
- **Line E** runs from Saint-Martin-le-Vinoux to Le Fontanil-Cornillon Palluel, expanding the network to the northern outskirts.

Trams operate from early morning until late at night, with reduced service during weekends and public holidays. Tickets can be purchased at tram stops, through the TAG app, or via ticket machines, and must be validated upon boarding.

Buses

The bus network complements the trams, reaching areas not served by tram lines. With over 40 routes, buses cover extensive ground, including the outer suburbs and neighboring towns. Key bus routes include the Chrono lines (C1, C2, C3, C4, and C5), which offer high-frequency service on major corridors.

Buses are particularly useful for accessing hiking trails and recreational areas in the surrounding mountains. Like the trams, bus tickets can be purchased and validated similarly, and schedules are available on the TAG website and app.

Cycling and Walking

Grenoble is renowned for its commitment to sustainable transportation, and cycling and walking are highly encouraged. The city has an extensive network of bike lanes and pedestrian paths, making it easy to navigate on foot or by bicycle.

Cycling

Grenoble's flat terrain in the city center and designated bike lanes make cycling a safe and enjoyable option. The city's bike-sharing program, Métrovélo, offers a convenient way to rent bikes. With over 7,000 bicycles available, including electric bikes, Métrovélo is one of the largest bike-sharing systems in France.

You can rent bikes from various locations around the city, including near major tram and bus stops. Short-term and long-term rental options are available, catering to both tourists and residents. Helmets and locks are provided, ensuring safety and security.

Popular cycling routes include the paths along the Isère River, offering scenic views and access to parks and gardens. For the more adventurous, the surrounding mountains provide challenging trails and stunning vistas.

Walking

Grenoble is highly walkable, especially within the city center. Many of the main attractions, such as the Grenoble Museum and Place Grenette, are within walking distance of each other. The old town, with its narrow, cobblestone streets, is best explored on foot.

Walking tours are a great way to discover Grenoble's history and culture. Guided tours are available, or you can explore at your own pace using self-guided tour apps and maps. Key walking routes include the path to the Bastille, which offers a rewarding hike with panoramic views of the city and the Alps.

Car Rentals and Taxis

While Grenoble's public transportation and cycling options are excellent, there are times when renting a car or taking a taxi may be more convenient, especially for trips outside the city.

Car Rentals

Several car rental agencies operate in Grenoble, including international brands like Hertz, Avis, and Europcar, as well as local companies. Rental offices are located at the train station, the airport, and various locations throughout the city.

Renting a car is ideal for exploring the wider Rhône-Alpes region, including the nearby ski resorts and natural parks. Be aware that driving in the city center can be challenging due to narrow streets and limited parking. Parking garages are available, but it's often easier to park on the outskirts and use public transportation to reach central areas.

Taxis

Taxis are readily available in Grenoble and can be hailed on the street, booked by phone, or reserved via apps like Uber and local taxi services. Taxi stands are located at major transport hubs, including the train station and popular tourist spots.

Taxis are a convenient option for airport transfers, late-night travel, or when carrying heavy luggage. Fares are metered, with additional charges for luggage and late-night service. It's advisable to check the fare estimate before starting your journey.

Accessibility in Grenoble

Grenoble is committed to being an inclusive city, and many efforts have been made to ensure accessibility for all. Public transportation is designed to accommodate passengers with reduced mobility, featuring low-floor trams and buses equipped with ramps and designated spaces for wheelchairs.

Key attractions, such as the Bastille, Musée de Grenoble, and major public buildings, have accessibility features, including ramps, elevators, and accessible restrooms. The city also provides detailed information on accessible routes and services through its tourist information centers and websites.

Hotels and restaurants in Grenoble are increasingly aware of accessibility needs, with many offering accessible rooms and facilities. When planning your visit, it's a good idea to check accessibility details in advance to ensure a smooth and enjoyable experience.

Grenoble's commitment to accessibility, combined with its efficient public transportation and extensive cycling and walking paths, makes it an easy city to navigate. Whether you prefer the convenience of trams and buses, the freedom of cycling, or the simplicity of walking, getting around Grenoble is both practical and enjoyable.

Chapter 4: Accommodation in Grenoble

Luxury Hotels

Grenoble offers a selection of luxurious accommodations that provide exceptional comfort, service, and amenities. These high-end hotels cater to discerning travelers seeking a refined and indulgent stay.

Le Grand Hôtel Grenoble Centre

Located in the heart of the city, Le Grand Hôtel Grenoble Centre combines elegance with modern amenities. This 4-star hotel boasts stylish rooms with plush bedding, marble bathrooms, and high-end toiletries. Guests can enjoy a gourmet breakfast buffet, a chic bar, and room service. The central location makes it ideal for exploring Grenoble's attractions, dining, and shopping.

- Address: 5 Rue de la République, 38000 Grenoble
- Website: [Le Grand Hôtel Grenoble Centre](https://www.grand-hotel-grenoble.com)

Hôtel Mercure Grenoble Centre Alpotel

Another excellent option for luxury accommodation is the Hôtel Mercure Grenoble Centre Alpotel. This 4-star hotel features contemporary rooms with comfortable furnishings, a restaurant offering regional cuisine, and a cozy bar. Business travelers will appreciate the meeting rooms and business services available.

- Address: 12 Boulevard Maréchal Joffre, 38000 Grenoble
- Website: [Hôtel Mercure Grenoble Centre Alpotel](https://all.accor.com/hotel/1177/index.en.shtml)

Park Hôtel Grenoble - MGallery

For a blend of historic charm and modern luxury, consider the Park Hôtel Grenoble - MGallery. This boutique hotel is set in a beautifully restored building and offers elegantly decorated rooms, a wellness center with a sauna and hammam, and an on-site restaurant serving gourmet dishes. Its proximity to Paul Mistral Park adds to its appeal.

- Address: 10 Place Paul Mistral, 38000 Grenoble
- Website: [Park Hôtel Grenoble - MGallery](https://all.accor.com/hotel/8613/index.en.shtml)

Mid-Range Hotels

Grenoble's mid-range hotels offer a balance of comfort, convenience, and value. These accommodations provide a range of amenities and are well-suited for both leisure and business travelers.

Ibis Styles Grenoble Centre Gare

The Ibis Styles Grenoble Centre Gare is a popular choice for travelers seeking affordable comfort. This hotel features bright and colorful rooms, complimentary breakfast, and free Wi-Fi. Its location near the train station makes it a convenient base for exploring the city and beyond.

- Address: 25 Avenue Félix Viallet, 38000 Grenoble
- Website: [Ibis Styles Grenoble Centre Gare](https://all.accor.com/hotel/7501/index.en.shtml)

Hôtel Europole

Hôtel Europole offers modern and spacious rooms with a minimalist design. The hotel includes a restaurant, bar, and fitness center, and it is conveniently located near the World Trade Center Grenoble and the train station, making it ideal for business travelers.

- Address: 29 Rue Pierre-Sémard, 38000 Grenoble
- Website: [Hôtel Europole](https://www.hotel-europole.com)

Okko Hotels Grenoble Jardin Hoche

Okko Hotels Grenoble Jardin Hoche combines stylish accommodation with a range of thoughtful amenities, including a fitness center, a shared lounge with free refreshments, and a breakfast buffet. The hotel's modern design and convenient location near the city's green spaces make it a great choice for travelers.

- Address: 23 Rue Hoche, 38000 Grenoble
- Website: [Okko Hotels Grenoble Jardin Hoche](https://www.okkohotels.com/en/hotels/grenoble)

Budget-Friendly Options

Grenoble has a variety of budget-friendly accommodations that provide comfort and essential amenities without breaking the bank. These options are perfect for travelers on a tight budget or those who prefer to spend more on activities and dining.

Résidhotel Grenette

Résidhotel Grenette offers affordable studio and apartment-style accommodations with kitchenettes, making it a great option for longer stays. The central location allows easy access to Grenoble's attractions, shops, and public transport.

- Address: 12 Rue de Palanka, 38000 Grenoble
- Website: [Résidhotel Grenette](https://www.residhotel.com/grenette)

Hôtel Alizé

Hôtel Alizé is a budget hotel located near the train station and the city center. It provides basic, clean rooms with free Wi-Fi and a continental breakfast. Its proximity to public transport makes it convenient for getting around Grenoble.

- Address: 1 Rue Amiral Courbet, 38000 Grenoble
- Website: [Hôtel Alizé](https://hotel-alize-grenoble.com)

B&B Hôtel Grenoble Centre Alpexpo

For budget-conscious travelers seeking modern amenities, the B&B Hôtel Grenoble Centre Alpexpo is a solid choice. This hotel offers comfortable rooms, free Wi-Fi, and a breakfast buffet at a reasonable price. It is located near the Alpexpo convention center and a tram stop.

- Address: 31 Avenue de l'Europe, 38100 Grenoble

- Website: [B&B Hôtel Grenoble Centre Alpexpo](https://www.hotel-bb.com/en/hotel/grenoble-centre-alpexpo)

Unique and Boutique Stays

For travelers looking for something a bit different, Grenoble offers unique and boutique accommodations that provide memorable experiences and personalized service.

Maison Barbillon Grenoble

Maison Barbillon Grenoble is a charming boutique hotel with a cozy and intimate atmosphere. Each room is individually decorated with a blend of vintage and contemporary styles. The hotel offers a delightful breakfast, a relaxing lounge area, and attentive service.

- Address: 10 Rue Louis Barbillon, 38000 Grenoble
- Website: [Maison Barbillon Grenoble](https://www.maisonbarbillon.com)

Hôtel d'Angleterre

Located in a historic building overlooking Place Victor Hugo, Hôtel d'Angleterre combines traditional elegance with modern comfort. The hotel features tastefully decorated rooms, a welcoming atmosphere, and an excellent location near the city's main attractions.

- Address: 5 Place Victor Hugo, 38000 Grenoble

- Website: [Hôtel d'Angleterre](https://www.hotel-angleterre-grenoble.com)

Le Hüb by Privilodges

Le Hüb by Privilodges offers a unique blend of hotel and hostel accommodations, with options ranging from private rooms to shared dormitories. The property includes communal spaces such as a kitchen, lounge, and coworking area, fostering a community atmosphere. Its central location makes it an ideal base for exploring Grenoble.

- Address: 25 Avenue Doyen Louis Weil, 38000 Grenoble
- Website: [Le Hüb by Privilodges](https://www.privilodges.com/en/hotel-apparthotel-grenoble/le-hub)

Grenoble's diverse range of accommodations ensures that every traveler can find the perfect place to stay, whether they seek luxury, comfort, affordability, or a unique experience.

Chapter 5: Must-See Sights

Bastille Fort

Perched atop the hills overlooking Grenoble, the Bastille Fort is an iconic symbol of the city and a must-visit attraction for any traveler. The fort offers a fascinating glimpse into Grenoble's military history, coupled with breathtaking panoramic views of the city and the surrounding Alps.

History and Significance

The Bastille Fort dates back to the 19th century, although the site has been used for military purposes since Roman times. Its strategic location made it a key defensive structure, and it played a crucial role in protecting Grenoble from potential invasions. Today, it stands as a testament to the city's rich historical heritage.

Visiting the Fort

Visitors can explore the well-preserved fortifications, including barracks, underground passages, and observation points. The fort also houses several exhibitions detailing its history and the broader military history of the region.

- Address: Montée Chalemont, 38000 Grenoble
- Website: [Bastille Grenoble](https://www.bastille-grenoble.fr)

Grenoble Museum (Musée de Grenoble)

The Grenoble Museum, or Musée de Grenoble, is one of the city's cultural highlights and a paradise for art lovers. This

42

renowned institution boasts an impressive collection of art spanning from antiquity to contemporary works.

Collection Highlights

The museum's collection includes masterpieces by renowned artists such as Picasso, Matisse, and Monet, alongside works from ancient Egypt and classical antiquity. The museum also features a substantial collection of modern and contemporary art, making it a comprehensive art destination.

Visiting Information

The Grenoble Museum is located in the heart of the city, making it easily accessible. It offers guided tours, workshops, and temporary exhibitions, providing a dynamic and enriching experience for visitors.

- Address: 5 Place de Lavalette, 38000 Grenoble
- Website: [Musée de Grenoble](https://www.museedegrenoble.fr)

Musée Dauphinois

Nestled on the slopes of the Bastille Hill, the Musée Dauphinois offers a captivating journey through the cultural and historical heritage of the Dauphiné region. Housed in a former convent, the museum provides a unique setting for its diverse exhibits.

Exhibitions and Collections
The museum's exhibits cover a wide range of topics, from traditional crafts and rural life to the history of skiing in the Alps. Interactive displays and multimedia presentations make the museum engaging for visitors of all ages.

Visiting Information

The Musée Dauphinois is surrounded by beautiful gardens and offers stunning views of Grenoble. Admission is typically free, making it an accessible cultural attraction for everyone.

- Address: 30 Rue Maurice Gignoux, 38000 Grenoble
- Website: [Musée Dauphinois](https://musees.isere.fr/musee/musee-dauphinois)

Paul Mistral Park

Paul Mistral Park is one of Grenoble's largest and most popular green spaces, offering a peaceful retreat from the city's hustle and bustle. The park is named after a former mayor of Grenoble and is a favorite spot for both locals and visitors.

Attractions and Activities

The park features expansive lawns, walking paths, and a variety of sports facilities, including a skate park, basketball courts, and a football field. It also hosts the Palais des Sports, an indoor arena for various events and performances.

Visiting Information

Paul Mistral Park is an ideal place for picnics, leisurely strolls, or outdoor activities. The park's central location makes it easily accessible, and it often serves as a venue for festivals and public events.

- Address: Boulevard Jean Pain, 38000 Grenoble
- Website: [Paul Mistral Park](https://www.grenoble.fr/100-parcs-et-jardins.htm)

Grenoble-Bastille Cable Car

The Grenoble-Bastille Cable Car, also known as Les Bulles, is one of the city's most distinctive and popular attractions. The cable car ride provides a thrilling ascent from the city center to the Bastille Fort, offering unparalleled views along the way.

The Experience

The cable car cabins, often referred to as "bubbles" due to their shape, offer a panoramic view of Grenoble, the Isère River, and the surrounding mountains. The ride lasts about five minutes and is an unforgettable way to reach the Bastille Fort.

Visiting Information

The cable car operates year-round, with extended hours during the summer months. It is easily accessible from the city center and is a must-do activity for visitors.

- Address: Quai Stéphane Jay, 38000 Grenoble
- Website: [Grenoble-Bastille Cable Car](https://www.bastille-grenoble.fr/en/les-bulles-grenoble-bastille-cable-car)

Archaeological Museum (Musée Archéologique Grenoble Saint-Laurent)

The Archaeological Museum of Grenoble, located in the ancient Saint-Laurent church, offers a fascinating look into the city's ancient past. The museum showcases a wealth of archaeological finds from Grenoble and the surrounding region.

Exhibitions and Highlights

Visitors can explore well-preserved artifacts, including Roman mosaics, medieval tombs, and religious relics. The museum's unique setting within a historic church adds to the sense of discovery.

Visiting Information

The Archaeological Museum is situated on the right bank of the Isère River, providing a scenic backdrop for your visit. The museum often hosts special exhibitions and educational programs.

- Address: Place Saint-Laurent, 38000 Grenoble
- Website: [Musée Archéologique Grenoble Saint-Laurent](https://musees.isere.fr/musee/musee-archeologique)

Grenoble's top attractions offer a diverse array of experiences, from exploring historical forts and museums to enjoying serene parks and thrilling cable car rides. Each site provides a unique insight into the city's rich heritage and vibrant culture, making Grenoble a compelling destination for travelers of all interests. Whether you're an art enthusiast, history buff, nature lover, or simply looking to soak in the stunning Alpine scenery, Grenoble has something to captivate and inspire you.

Chapter 6 Exploring Grenoble's Quarters

City Center

Grenoble's City Center is the vibrant heart of the city, combining historic charm with modern amenities. This bustling area is packed with shops, restaurants, cafes, and cultural attractions, making it an essential destination for any visitor.

Key Attractions

The City Center is home to the Place Grenette, a lively square surrounded by cafes and shops. Here, you can relax with a coffee and people-watch, or explore the nearby pedestrian streets filled with boutiques and local businesses. The Jardin de Ville, a beautiful city garden, offers a peaceful respite with its manicured lawns, flower beds, and shaded benches.

Shopping and Dining

Grenoble's City Center boasts a diverse shopping scene, from high-end fashion stores to quaint local shops. Rue de Bonne and Rue Félix Poulat are particularly popular for their variety of stores. For dining, you'll find everything from traditional French bistros to international cuisine, ensuring there's something to suit every palate.

Cultural Highlights

The City Center is also rich in cultural landmarks. Don't miss the Grenoble Museum (Musée de Grenoble), which features an impressive collection of art from antiquity to the present. The historic Grenoble Cathedral, with its stunning Gothic architecture, is another must-see.

- Address: Place Grenette, 38000 Grenoble
- Website: [Grenoble Tourism](https://www.grenoble-tourisme.com)

Quartier Saint-Laurent

Quartier Saint-Laurent is one of Grenoble's oldest and most picturesque neighborhoods. Located on the right bank of the Isère River, this area is known for its narrow cobblestone streets, historic buildings, and vibrant atmosphere.

Historic Significance

This quarter has a rich history, dating back to Roman times. The Archaeological Museum of Grenoble (Musée Archéologique Grenoble Saint-Laurent), housed in the ancient Saint-Laurent church, offers fascinating insights into the area's past. Here, you can explore Roman mosaics, medieval tombs, and other archaeological finds.

Local Life and Atmosphere

Quartier Saint-Laurent is a lively area with a bohemian vibe. It's known for its eclectic mix of cafes, bars, and restaurants, many of which offer stunning views of the river and the Bastille Fort. The neighborhood's artistic flair is evident in its street art and independent galleries.

Highlights

Stroll along the Quai Xavier Jouvin for scenic river views and explore the charming side streets to discover hidden gems. The Saint-Laurent Bridge, with its picturesque arches, is a great spot for a photo op.

- Address: Place Saint-Laurent, 38000 Grenoble
- Website: [Musée Archéologique Grenoble Saint-Laurent](https://musees.isere.fr/musee/musee-archeologique)

Île Verte

Île Verte, or "Green Island," is a tranquil residential district located north of the city center. Known for its green spaces and peaceful ambiance, Île Verte is an ideal place to relax and enjoy nature within the city.

Green Spaces and Parks

As its name suggests, Île Verte is home to several parks and gardens. The Parc Île Verte is a lovely green space perfect for leisurely strolls, picnics, and outdoor activities. The neighborhood's tree-lined streets and well-maintained gardens contribute to its serene atmosphere.

Residential Charm

Île Verte is primarily a residential area, with charming houses and apartment buildings. It offers a glimpse into everyday life in Grenoble, away from the hustle and bustle of the more touristy areas. The neighborhood is well-connected by public transport, making it easy to reach from other parts of the city.

Highlights

The tranquil environment of Île Verte makes it a great place for a leisurely walk or bike ride. The neighborhood's proximity to the Isère River also provides opportunities for riverside walks and enjoying the natural beauty of the area.

- Address: Île Verte, 38000 Grenoble
- Website: [Grenoble Tourism](https://www.grenoble-tourisme.com)

Europole

Europole is Grenoble's modern business district, located near the train station and the World Trade Center. This dynamic area is characterized by its contemporary architecture, corporate offices, and conference facilities.

Business Hub
Europole is the epicenter of Grenoble's business and tech industries. The area is home to numerous corporate headquarters, research centers, and start-ups, making it a vital part of the city's economy. The World Trade Center Grenoble, a prominent venue for conferences and events, is located here.

Modern Amenities
Despite its business focus, Europole offers a range of amenities for visitors. You'll find modern hotels, cafes, and restaurants catering to business travelers and locals alike. The area is also well-connected, with easy access to public transport, including trams and buses.

Highlights
For those interested in science and innovation, the nearby Grenoble Science Centre (La Casemate) offers interactive

exhibits and workshops. Europole's contemporary architecture, with its sleek glass and steel buildings, provides a striking contrast to Grenoble's historic quarters.

- Address: Europole, 38000 Grenoble
- Website: [World Trade Center Grenoble](https://www.wtc-grenoble.com)

Presqu'île

The Presqu'île district, also known as the Peninsula, is an emerging area in Grenoble, undergoing significant development and transformation. Located between the Isère River and the Drac River, this district is becoming a hub for innovation and sustainability.

Innovation and Development
Presqu'île is home to the GIANT (Grenoble Innovation for Advanced New Technologies) campus, a leading center for research and development. The campus includes various research institutions, technology companies, and educational facilities, driving innovation in fields such as energy, health, and information technology.

Sustainable Living
The district's development emphasizes sustainability and quality of life. New residential areas feature eco-friendly buildings, green spaces, and community facilities. The neighborhood is designed to promote walking, cycling, and public transport use, reducing reliance on cars.

Highlights

One of the district's highlights is the Minatec campus, a center for micro and nanotechnology research. Visitors can also enjoy the newly developed parks and public spaces, which provide a pleasant environment for relaxation and recreation.

- Address: Presqu'île, 38000 Grenoble
- Website: [GIANT Campus](https://www.giant-grenoble.org)

Grenoble's diverse neighborhoods and districts offer a rich tapestry of experiences, from the historic charm of Quartier Saint-Laurent to the modern innovation of Europole and Presqu'île. Each area has its own unique character and attractions, providing visitors with a comprehensive and engaging exploration of the city. Whether you're interested in history, culture, nature, or business, Grenoble's quarters have something special to offer, making your visit both memorable and enriching.

Chapter 7: Cultural Experiences

Art, Music, and Theater

Grenoble boasts a vibrant cultural scene that caters to art lovers, music enthusiasts, and theater aficionados. The city is home to numerous art galleries, performing arts venues, and hosts a variety of music festivals and annual events that showcase its rich cultural heritage.

Art Galleries

Grenoble's art galleries offer a diverse range of exhibitions, from classical works to contemporary pieces, providing visitors with an enriching visual experience.

Musée de Grenoble

The Musée de Grenoble is the city's premier art museum, featuring an extensive collection that spans from antiquity to the modern era. With masterpieces from artists such as Picasso, Matisse, and Kandinsky, the museum is a must-visit for art enthusiasts.

- Address: 5 Place de Lavalette, 38000 Grenoble
- Website: [Musée de Grenoble](https://www.museedegrenoble.fr)

Magasin - Centre National d'Art Contemporain

Housed in a former industrial warehouse, Magasin is one of France's largest centers for contemporary art. It features rotating exhibitions by both emerging and established artists, along with workshops and cultural events.

- Address: Site Bouchayer-Viallet, 155 Cours Berriat, 38000 Grenoble
- Website: [Magasin - CNAC](http://www.magasin-cnac.org)

Galerie Vent des Cimes

For those interested in contemporary and modern art, Galerie Vent des Cimes offers a variety of works from local and international artists. The gallery specializes in painting, sculpture, and photography, providing a dynamic cultural experience.

- Address: 25 Avenue Alsace-Lorraine, 38000 Grenoble
- Website: [Galerie Vent des Cimes](http://www.ventdescimes.com)

Performing Arts Venues

Grenoble's performing arts scene is vibrant and diverse, with venues hosting everything from classical theater to cutting-edge performances.

La MC2: Maison de la Culture

La MC2 is Grenoble's largest cultural venue, hosting a wide range of performances, including theater, dance, music, and opera. The center is known for its high-quality productions and often features international acts.

- Address: 4 Rue Paul Claudel, 38100 Grenoble
- Website: [La MC2](https://www.mc2grenoble.fr)

Théâtre de Grenoble

The Théâtre de Grenoble, also known as Théâtre 145, offers a variety of theatrical performances, from classic plays to contemporary works. The intimate setting provides a unique experience for theatergoers.

- Address: 145 Rue Pierre Duclot, 38000 Grenoble
- Website: [Théâtre de Grenoble](https://www.theatredegrenoble.com)

L'Ampérage

For a more alternative scene, L'Ampérage is a popular venue for independent music and performance art. It hosts concerts, DJ sets, and avant-garde performances, making it a hub for Grenoble's creative community.

- Address: 163 Cours Berriat, 38000 Grenoble
- Website: [L'Ampérage](https://www.amperage.fr)

Music Festivals

Grenoble's music festivals offer something for every taste, from classical to contemporary music. These events draw visitors from all over and highlight the city's rich musical heritage.

Festival de Musique de Chambre

The Festival de Musique de Chambre (Chamber Music Festival) is a highlight of Grenoble's cultural calendar. Held annually, the festival features performances by renowned chamber musicians in various historic venues throughout the city.

- Website: [Festival de Musique de Chambre](https://www.festival-musique-chambre.fr)

Cabaret Frappé

Cabaret Frappé is a summer music festival that transforms Grenoble's Jardin de Ville into a lively concert venue. The festival showcases a wide range of genres, from rock and pop to jazz and electronic music, and is known for its vibrant atmosphere.

- Website: [Cabaret Frappé](https://www.cabaret-frappe.com)

Les Détours de Babel

Les Détours de Babel is an innovative festival that explores the intersections of contemporary music and global cultures. The festival includes concerts, workshops, and lectures, offering a unique cultural experience.

- Website: [Les Détours de Babel](https://www.detoursdebabel.fr)

Annual Events

Grenoble's annual events celebrate its cultural diversity and community spirit, providing visitors with unique opportunities to experience local traditions and festivities.

Fête des Lumières

Inspired by Lyon's famous festival, Grenoble's Fête des Lumières (Festival of Lights) illuminates the city with stunning light installations and projections. The event takes place in December and transforms Grenoble into a magical wonderland.

- Website: [Fête des Lumières Grenoble](https://www.grenoble-tourisme.com)

Festival du Film Court en Plein Air

The Festival du Film Court en Plein Air (Outdoor Short Film Festival) is one of the oldest short film festivals in France. Held in July, it features screenings of short films from around the world in various outdoor locations across the city.

- Website: [Festival du Film Court en Plein Air](https://www.festival-grenoble.com)

Marché de Noël

Grenoble's Christmas Market, or Marché de Noël, is a festive highlight of the winter season. Held in Place Victor Hugo, the market features dozens of stalls selling holiday treats, crafts, and gifts, along with live entertainment and activities for all ages.

- Website: [Marché de Noël Grenoble](https://www.grenoble-tourisme.com)

Grenoble's rich cultural scene offers a wealth of experiences for visitors. From its prestigious art galleries and dynamic performing arts venues to its lively music festivals and annual events, the city is a hub of creativity and artistic expression. Whether you're an art lover, a music enthusiast, or simply looking to immerse yourself in the local culture, Grenoble has something to offer every visitor, making it a must-visit destination for cultural exploration.

Chapter 8: Embracing Nature

Grenoble, nestled in the French Alps, offers an array of outdoor activities that cater to nature enthusiasts and adventure seekers. From hiking trails and cycling routes to skiing and snowboarding, the city and its surroundings provide numerous opportunities for exploring the great outdoors.

Hiking Trails

Grenoble's location at the foot of the Alps makes it an ideal base for hiking. The surrounding mountains offer a variety of trails suitable for all levels of experience.

Chartreuse Mountains

The Chartreuse Mountains, to the east of Grenoble, provide stunning hiking opportunities. The Circuit des Crêtes, a popular trail, offers breathtaking panoramic views of the surrounding valleys and peaks. The hike is moderately challenging and is perfect for those seeking a full-day adventure.

- Trailhead: Col de Porte, 38700 Saint-Pierre-de-Chartreuse
- Website: [Parc Naturel Régional de Chartreuse](https://www.chartreuse.fr)

Vercors Regional Natural Park

To the south of Grenoble, the Vercors Regional Natural Park features numerous hiking trails. The Gorges de la Bourne Trail is a standout, offering spectacular views of dramatic gorges and river valleys. This trail is suitable for intermediate hikers and provides a great way to experience the park's rugged terrain.

- Trailhead: Pont-en-Royans, 38680
- Website: [Parc Naturel Régional du Vercors](https://www.parc-du-vercors.fr)

Belledonne Range

The Belledonne Range, located to the northeast of Grenoble, offers more challenging hikes. The Grand Serre Trail, which ascends to one of the range's highest peaks, provides spectacular alpine scenery and a rewarding experience for experienced hikers.

- Trailhead: Les Clavaux, 38580 Allevard
- Website: [Massif de Belledonne](https://www.belledonne.fr)

Cycling Routes

Grenoble is also a great destination for cycling enthusiasts, with a variety of routes that cater to different skill levels.

La Véloroute du Val de Drôme

This scenic route follows the Drôme River and is ideal for a leisurely bike ride. The route passes through charming villages, vineyards, and lush landscapes, offering a relaxing way to explore the region.

- Route: From Crest to Valence
- Website: [Véloroute du Val de Drôme](https://www.valdedrome.com)

Grenoble to Lake Geneva

For a more challenging ride, consider the route from Grenoble to Lake Geneva. This route takes cyclists through picturesque Alpine scenery and includes a climb over the Col du Glandon. It's recommended for experienced cyclists seeking a longer, demanding ride.

- Route: Grenoble to Thonon-les-Bains
- Website: [Cycling in the Alps](https://www.cycling-alps.com)

Bike Paths in Grenoble

Grenoble itself offers several dedicated bike paths, such as the Isère River Path. This path runs along the river and provides a scenic, flat route perfect for casual cycling.

- Path: Along the Isère River
- Website: [Grenoble Bike Paths](https://www.grenoble.fr)

Skiing and Snowboarding

During the winter months, Grenoble becomes a gateway to some of the best skiing and snowboarding resorts in the French Alps.

Alpe d'Huez

Located about 100 km from Grenoble, Alpe d'Huez is renowned for its extensive ski terrain and sunny weather. The resort features over 250 km of ski slopes suitable for all skill levels and is known for its vibrant après-ski scene.

- Location: Alpe d'Huez, 38750
- Website: [Alpe d'Huez](https://www.alpedhuez.com)

Les Deux Alpes

Another popular destination, Les Deux Alpes is approximately 90 km from Grenoble. It offers one of the largest skiable glaciers in Europe, providing excellent conditions for skiing and snowboarding throughout the season.

- Location: Les Deux Alpes, 38860
- Website: [Les Deux Alpes](https://www.les2alpes.com)

Chamrousse

Closer to Grenoble, Chamrousse is known for its family-friendly slopes and stunning views. The resort is ideal for both beginners and advanced skiers and offers a more relaxed atmosphere compared to the larger resorts.

- Location: Chamrousse, 38410
- Website: [Chamrousse](https://www.chamrousse.com)

Parks and Gardens

Grenoble's parks and gardens provide tranquil escapes from the urban environment, offering opportunities for relaxation and outdoor activities.

Jardin de Ville

Located in the heart of Grenoble, the Jardin de Ville is a beautifully landscaped park with wide lawns, flower beds, and shaded walkways. It's a perfect spot for a picnic or a leisurely stroll.

- Address: Place de Lavalette, 38000 Grenoble
- Website: [Jardin de Ville](https://www.grenoble.fr)

Parc Paul Mistral

One of the largest parks in Grenoble, Parc Paul Mistral offers extensive green spaces, sports facilities, and playgrounds. The park is an excellent place for outdoor sports, jogging, or simply enjoying nature.

- Address: 30 Avenue de Constantine, 38000 Grenoble
- Website: [Parc Paul Mistral](https://www.grenoble.fr)

Water Sports

Grenoble's location near rivers and lakes provides opportunities for various water sports, including kayaking, rafting, and paddleboarding.

Isère River

The Isère River, which runs through Grenoble, is a popular spot for kayaking and rafting. Several local companies offer equipment rentals and guided tours for adventurers looking to explore the river's rapids and scenic surroundings.

- Location: Various access points along the river
- Website: [Grenoble Rafting](https://www.grenoble-rafting.com)

Lac de Monteynard

Approximately 50 km from Grenoble, Lac de Monteynard is a stunning lake ideal for paddleboarding, sailing, and windsurfing. The lake's clear waters and picturesque setting make it a favorite destination for water sports enthusiasts.

- Location: Monteynard, 38770
- Website: [Lac de Monteynard](https://www.lac-monteynard.fr)

Grenoble's natural surroundings offer a wide range of outdoor activities that cater to every interest and skill level. Whether you're hiking in the nearby mountains, cycling along scenic routes, skiing in the Alps, or enjoying the city's parks and water sports, Grenoble provides ample opportunities to embrace nature and experience the great outdoors. The city's blend of urban convenience and natural beauty ensures that every visitor can find an adventure that suits their preferences.

Chapter 9: Retail Therapy

Grenoble offers a diverse shopping experience that caters to all tastes and preferences. From bustling local markets and modern shopping centers to charming boutiques and specialty shops, the city provides ample opportunities for retail therapy. Whether you're looking for unique souvenirs or local crafts, Grenoble has something for everyone.

Local Markets

Local markets in Grenoble are vibrant hubs of activity where you can explore a variety of fresh produce, artisanal goods, and regional specialties. These markets provide an authentic taste of the local culture and offer a chance to interact with local vendors.

Marché des Halles Sainte-Claire

The Marché des Halles Sainte-Claire is one of Grenoble's most famous markets. Located in the heart of the city, this covered market features a wide range of stalls selling fresh produce, cheeses, meats, and baked goods. It's a great place to experience local flavors and pick up some gourmet ingredients.

- Address: Place Sainte-Claire, 38000 Grenoble
- Opening Hours: Tuesday to Saturday, 7:00 AM - 1:00 PM

Marché de l'Estacade

The Marché de l'Estacade is a lively open-air market held in the Estacade neighborhood. It offers a variety of goods, including fresh fruits and vegetables, flowers, and household items. The market is known for its friendly atmosphere and is popular among locals.

- Address: Place de l'Estacade, 38100 Grenoble
- Opening Hours: Thursday and Sunday, 7:00 AM - 1:00 PM

Marché de Bérivière

Located in the Bérivière district, this market focuses on organic and locally produced products. It's an excellent spot for those looking for fresh, sustainable options and artisanal goods. The market also features craft stalls and food trucks.

- Address: Place de Bérivière, 38000 Grenoble
- Opening Hours: Saturday, 8:00 AM - 1:00 PM

Shopping Centers

For a more conventional shopping experience, Grenoble has several shopping centers where you can find a mix of high-street brands, specialty stores, and dining options.

Grand'Place

Grand'Place is one of the largest shopping centers in Grenoble, offering a wide range of stores, including fashion retailers, electronics shops, and home goods stores. The center also features a food court with various dining options, making it a convenient destination for a shopping spree.

- Address: 14 Avenue d'Innsbruck, 38100 Grenoble
- Opening Hours: Monday to Saturday, 10:00 AM - 7:00 PM

Carrefour Grenoble Cité

Carrefour Grenoble Cité is a large hypermarket that combines a supermarket with a selection of retail shops. It's a one-stop-shop for groceries, clothing, electronics, and more. The center also has a variety of restaurants and cafes.

- Address: 10 Avenue de l'Europe, 38100 Grenoble
- Opening Hours: Monday to Saturday, 9:00 AM - 8:00 PM

Centre Commercial La Tronche

Located just outside the city center, Centre Commercial La Tronche offers a range of stores and services. It includes both large chain stores and smaller boutiques, providing a balanced shopping experience.

- Address: 11 Route de la Tronche, 38700 La Tronche
- Opening Hours: Monday to Saturday, 10:00 AM - 7:00 PM

Boutiques and Specialty Shops

Grenoble's charming boutiques and specialty shops offer unique items that you won't find in larger chain stores. These shops are perfect for finding distinctive fashion pieces, handcrafted goods, and local treasures.

L'Atelier de la Mode

L'Atelier de la Mode is a boutique known for its curated selection of high-quality fashion items. The store features both French and international designers, offering everything from elegant evening wear to stylish everyday outfits.

- Address: 12 Rue de Strasbourg, 38000 Grenoble
- Website: [L'Atelier de la Mode](https://www.atelier-mode-grenoble.com)

Le Comptoir de la Malle

For unique vintage finds, Le Comptoir de la Malle offers a selection of antique and retro items, including clothing, accessories, and home decor. The boutique's eclectic collection makes it a great spot for those looking for something special.

- Address: 27 Rue Général Ferrié, 38000 Grenoble
- Website: [Le Comptoir de la Malle](https://www.comptoir-malle.com)

Maison du Chocolat

Maison du Chocolat is a specialty shop dedicated to high-quality chocolates and confections. The store offers a range of gourmet chocolates, pastries, and gift items, making it a perfect place to indulge or find a sweet gift.

- Address: 8 Rue de la République, 38000 Grenoble

- Website: [Maison du Chocolat](https://www.chocolat-grenoble.com)

Souvenirs and Local Crafts

Grenoble offers various options for souvenirs and local crafts, allowing visitors to take home a piece of the city's charm.

Les Artisans du Monde

Les Artisans du Monde specializes in fair-trade crafts and goods from around the world. The store features handmade items, including textiles, pottery, and jewelry, offering a unique selection of souvenirs.

- Address: 14 Rue de la République, 38000 Grenoble
- Website: [Les Artisans du Monde](https://www.artisansdumonde.org)

Boutique du Musée de Grenoble

Located within the Musée de Grenoble, this boutique offers a range of art-inspired souvenirs and gifts. You can find art prints, books, and decorative items that reflect the museum's collection and the city's artistic heritage.

- Address: 5 Place de Lavalette, 38000 Grenoble
- Website: [Boutique du Musée de Grenoble](https://www.museedegrenoble.fr)

La Boutique de la Maison de la Culture

La Boutique de la Maison de la Culture offers a variety of cultural and artistic items, including books, music, and local crafts. It's a great place to find unique gifts that celebrate Grenoble's cultural scene.

- Address: 4 Rue Paul Claudel, 38100 Grenoble
- Website: [La Boutique de la Maison de la Culture](https://www.mc2grenoble.fr)

Grenoble provides a rich shopping experience that ranges from bustling local markets and modern shopping centers to charming boutiques and specialty shops. Whether you're looking for fresh produce, unique fashion, or distinctive souvenirs, the city's diverse shopping scene ensures that there is something for everyone. Exploring Grenoble's retail offerings is not only an enjoyable experience but also a great way to connect with the local culture and bring home a piece of the city.

Chapter 10: Gastronomic Delights

Grenoble, nestled in the heart of the French Alps, is a culinary haven offering a rich tapestry of flavors. From traditional Alpine dishes to fine dining experiences, the city boasts a diverse array of dining options. Whether you're seeking classic French cuisine, cozy bistros, or innovative vegetarian and vegan fare, Grenoble has something to satisfy every palate. Local wineries and breweries also add to the city's vibrant gastronomic scene, providing an opportunity to sample regional wines and craft beers.

Traditional Alpine Dishes

The cuisine of the Alps is hearty and comforting, perfect for replenishing energy after a day of exploring the mountains. Traditional Alpine dishes are characterized by their use of local ingredients and time-honored cooking methods.

Fondue Savoyarde

Fondue Savoyarde is a classic Alpine dish made with a blend of cheeses, such as Gruyère, Emmental, and Comté, melted with white wine and garlic. This rich, creamy dish is served with chunks of crusty bread for dipping. Several restaurants in Grenoble specialize in this traditional favorite.

Restaurant Recommendation: La Table de l'Ours
- Address: 22 Rue des Vieilles Legendes, 38000 Grenoble
- Website: [La Table de l'Ours](https://www.latabledelours.com)

Raclette

Raclette is another Alpine specialty that features melted cheese scraped over boiled potatoes, pickles, and cured meats. It's a communal dish often enjoyed with friends and family. For an authentic experience, try this dish at one of Grenoble's traditional restaurants.

Restaurant Recommendation: Le Chalet Savoyard
- Address: 10 Rue du Général Ferrié, 38000 Grenoble
- Website: [Le Chalet Savoyard](https://www.chaletsavoyard.com)

Tartiflette

Tartiflette is a comforting casserole made with potatoes, Reblochon cheese, lardons (bacon), and onions. This dish is particularly popular during the winter months and offers a hearty taste of the Alps.

Restaurant Recommendation: L'Auberge de la Fontaine
- Address: 5 Place Notre-Dame, 38000 Grenoble
- Website: [L'Auberge de la Fontaine](https://www.aubergedelafontaine.com)

Fine Dining Restaurants

Grenoble is home to several fine dining establishments that offer refined culinary experiences with a focus on high-quality ingredients and sophisticated preparation techniques.

Le Fantin Latour

Le Fantin Latour is a Michelin-starred restaurant known for its elegant French cuisine and exceptional service. The menu features seasonal dishes crafted from locally sourced ingredients, and the wine list includes selections from top French vineyards.

- Address: 5 Rue de la Croix Rouge, 38000 Grenoble
- Website: [Le Fantin Latour](https://www.fantin-latour.com)

Le Gavroche

Le Gavroche offers a gourmet dining experience with a menu that combines traditional French flavors with modern techniques. The restaurant is renowned for its attention to detail and exquisite presentation.

- Address: 22 Rue de Strasbourg, 38000 Grenoble
- Website: [Le Gavroche](https://www.gavroche-grenoble.com)

Le Bistrot de l'Artisan

Le Bistrot de l'Artisan focuses on artisanal cuisine with a creative twist. The restaurant prides itself on using fresh, locally sourced ingredients to create innovative dishes that showcase the best of French gastronomy.

- Address: 14 Rue des Remparts, 38000 Grenoble

- Website: [Le Bistrot de l'Artisan](https://www.bistro-artisan.com)

Bistros and Cafés

Grenoble's bistros and cafés offer a more casual dining experience, perfect for enjoying a relaxed meal or a leisurely coffee break. These establishments are known for their friendly atmospheres and diverse menus.

Café de l'Industrie

Café de l'Industrie is a popular spot for a casual meal or coffee. The menu features a range of French dishes, including sandwiches, salads, and daily specials. It's a great place to unwind and enjoy the local ambiance.

- Address: 11 Boulevard Agutte Sembat, 38000 Grenoble
- Website: [Café de l'Industrie](https://www.cafedelindustrie.com)

Le Comptoir du Marché

Le Comptoir du Marché is a charming bistro offering traditional French fare in a cozy setting. The menu includes a variety of classic dishes, such as quiches, omelets, and charcuterie boards.

- Address: 8 Place de la Bastille, 38000 Grenoble
- Website: [Le Comptoir du Marché](https://www.comptoir-marche.com)

La Brasserie de la Gare

Located near the train station, La Brasserie de la Gare serves a range of French and international dishes. It's a convenient choice for travelers and locals alike, offering hearty meals and a welcoming atmosphere.

- Address: 1 Rue de la Gare, 38000 Grenoble
- Website: [La Brasserie de la Gare](https://www.brasserie-gare.com)

Vegetarian and Vegan Options

Grenoble has a growing selection of restaurants catering to vegetarian and vegan diets. These establishments focus on innovative dishes that highlight fresh, plant-based ingredients.

L'Artichaut

L'Artichaut is a dedicated vegetarian restaurant that offers a diverse menu of plant-based dishes. The restaurant's creative approach to vegetarian cuisine ensures that every meal is both flavorful and satisfying.

- Address: 12 Rue des Renaud, 38000 Grenoble
- Website: [L'Artichaut](https://www.artichaut-vegetarien.com)

Le Vieux Fusil

Le Vieux Fusil provides a range of vegan options alongside its traditional French fare. The restaurant's menu includes inventive vegan dishes, such as vegetable stews and tofu-based entrées.

- Address: 22 Rue des Tables, 38000 Grenoble
- Website: [Le Vieux Fusil](https://www.vieuxfusil-vegan.com)

Greenhouse Café

Greenhouse Café offers a variety of vegan and vegetarian dishes in a relaxed café setting. The menu features fresh salads, grain bowls, and smoothies, making it a great spot for a healthy and delicious meal.

- Address: 5 Rue des Ecoles, 38000 Grenoble
- Website: [Greenhouse Café](https://www.greenhouse-cafe.com)

Local Wineries and Breweries

Grenoble's surrounding regions are known for their excellent wines and craft beers. Local wineries and breweries offer opportunities to sample regional specialties and experience the area's rich beverage traditions.

Domaine de la Côte

Domaine de la Côte is a local winery that produces a range of wines from the surrounding Alpine vineyards. Visitors can enjoy tastings and tours, learning about the winemaking process and the unique characteristics of the region's wines.

- Address: 18 Route du Vin, 38700 La Tronche
- Website: [Domaine de la Côte](https://www.domainelacote.com)

Brasserie du Mont Blanc

Brasserie du Mont Blanc is a craft brewery that offers a selection of beers brewed using traditional methods. The brewery's beers are inspired by the Alpine landscape and include a variety of styles, from lagers to IPAs.

- Address: 21 Rue du Mont Blanc, 38100 Grenoble
- Website: [Brasserie du Mont Blanc](https://www.brasserie-montblanc.com)

Vignoble de Grenoble

The Vignoble de Grenoble focuses on producing high-quality wines from local grape varieties. The vineyard offers tastings and tours, providing insight into the region's winemaking heritage.

- Address: 14 Avenue de la Vigne, 38000 Grenoble
- Website: [Vignoble de Grenoble](https://www.vignoble-grenoble.com)

Grenoble's dining scene reflects the city's rich cultural heritage and diverse culinary influences. From traditional Alpine dishes and elegant fine dining to cozy bistros and innovative vegetarian options, there is something to please every palate. The local wineries and breweries further enhance the city's gastronomic landscape, offering a taste of the region's exceptional beverages. Whether you're indulging in classic French cuisine or exploring new flavors, Grenoble provides a memorable culinary experience.

Chapter 11: Evening Adventures

Grenoble offers a vibrant nightlife scene with a variety of options for evening entertainment. Whether you're looking to enjoy a casual drink at a bar, dance the night away at a nightclub, catch a live music performance, or experience a cultural event, the city provides something for every taste. Here's a guide to Grenoble's nightlife and entertainment, ensuring that your evenings are as engaging and enjoyable as your days.

Bars and Pubs

Grenoble's bars and pubs offer a relaxed atmosphere where you can unwind with a drink, enjoy good company, and experience the local social scene.

Le Bar du Bureau

Le Bar du Bureau is a popular spot for after-work drinks and casual gatherings. Known for its wide selection of beers, cocktails, and a laid-back vibe, it's a great place to start your evening. The bar also features board games and occasional live music.

- Address: 14 Rue de Strasbourg, 38000 Grenoble
- Website: [Le Bar du Bureau](https://www.bardubureau.com)

La Maison de la Biere

For beer enthusiasts, La Maison de la Biere offers an impressive selection of craft beers from local breweries and around the world. The pub's knowledgeable staff can help you find the perfect brew, and the cozy atmosphere makes it a favorite among locals.

- Address: 7 Rue de la Poste, 38000 Grenoble
- Website: [La Maison de la Biere](https://www.maison-biere-grenoble.com)

Le Comptoir des Alpes

Le Comptoir des Alpes is a charming bar that emphasizes local wines and artisanal spirits. The bar's rustic decor and friendly service create a welcoming environment, making it a great place to enjoy a glass of wine or a cocktail.

- Address: 22 Boulevard Agutte Sembat, 38000 Grenoble
- Website: [Le Comptoir des Alpes](https://www.comptoir-alpes.com)

Nightclubs

For those looking to dance and enjoy a lively atmosphere, Grenoble's nightclubs offer a range of options from high-energy dance floors to more relaxed lounges.

Le Club 360

Le Club 360 is one of Grenoble's premier nightclubs, featuring a state-of-the-art sound system and a spacious dance floor. The club hosts themed nights and DJ sets, making it a hotspot for both locals and visitors looking to experience the city's nightlife.

- Address: 10 Rue de la République, 38000 Grenoble

- Website: [Le Club 360](https://www.club360-grenoble.com)

La Belle Époque

La Belle Époque combines elegance with modern nightlife, offering a chic setting for an evening out. The club features a stylish interior, a variety of music genres, and a dedicated area for VIP guests.

- Address: 34 Rue de la Croix-Rouge, 38000 Grenoble
- Website: [La Belle Époque](https://www.belle-epoque-grenoble.com)

Le Fizz

Le Fizz is known for its eclectic mix of music and lively atmosphere. With regular DJ performances and themed parties, it's a popular choice for those looking to dance the night away in a vibrant setting.

- Address: 18 Rue Paul Claudel, 38100 Grenoble
- Website: [Le Fizz](https://www.fizz-grenoble.com)

Live Music Venues

Grenoble's live music venues showcase a range of musical styles, from local bands to international acts. Whether you're into jazz, rock, or classical music, there's a venue that caters to your tastes.

La Belle Electrique

La Belle Electrique is a modern music venue known for its diverse lineup of concerts and events. The venue hosts performances across various genres, including electronic, rock, and world music. Its cutting-edge facilities and intimate setting make it a favorite among music enthusiasts.

- Address: 21 Boulevard de l'Oisans, 38000 Grenoble
- Website: [La Belle Electrique](https://www.labelleelectrique.com)

Le 38 Riv' Café

Le 38 Riv' Café is a lively spot that features regular live music performances, including jazz, blues, and acoustic sets. The café's relaxed atmosphere and excellent sound quality make it a great place to enjoy live music while sipping on a drink.

- Address: 10 Rue des Écoles, 38000 Grenoble
- Website: [Le 38 Riv' Café](https://www.38rivcafe.com)

L'Antre-Peaux

L'Antre-Peaux is a cozy venue that focuses on showcasing emerging artists and local talent. The intimate setting allows for close interaction with performers, making it a great place to discover new music.

- Address: 5 Rue des Alliés, 38000 Grenoble

- Website: [L'Antre-Peaux](https://www.antrepeaux.com)

Cultural Nights

Grenoble also offers a range of cultural nights and events that provide a unique and enriching experience. From theater performances to film screenings, these events offer a chance to engage with the city's cultural scene.

Théâtre de Grenoble

Théâtre de Grenoble is a major cultural institution that hosts a variety of theatrical performances, including contemporary plays, classical works, and experimental theater. The theater's diverse program ensures that there's always something interesting to see.

- Address: 4 Rue Louis Barre, 38000 Grenoble
- Website: [Théâtre de Grenoble](https://www.theatre-grenoble.com)

Le Magasin – Centre National d'Art Contemporain

Le Magasin is a contemporary art center that hosts exhibitions, performances, and workshops. It's an ideal destination for those interested in modern art and cultural events. The center's dynamic program includes regular events that highlight innovative artistic practices.

- Address: 8 Esplanade Andry-Farcy, 38000 Grenoble

- Website: [Le Magasin](https://www.magasin-cnac.org)

Grenoble International Film Festival

The Grenoble International Film Festival is an annual event that showcases a wide range of films from around the world. The festival includes screenings, discussions, and workshops, offering an opportunity to explore international cinema in a vibrant setting.

- Address: Various locations in Grenoble
- Website: [Grenoble International Film Festival](https://www.festivalfilmgrenoble.com)

Grenoble's nightlife and entertainment scene offers a diverse range of experiences, ensuring that there is something for everyone to enjoy. From lively bars and nightclubs to intimate live music venues and enriching cultural events, the city provides numerous opportunities to explore and enjoy its vibrant social life. Whether you're looking for a relaxed evening out or an energetic night on the town, Grenoble has the perfect option to suit your preferences.

Chapter 12: Exploring Beyond Grenoble

Grenoble's central location in the French Alps makes it an ideal base for exploring the surrounding region. From picturesque mountain ranges to vibrant cities, there are numerous day trips and excursions that offer a taste of the diverse landscapes and cultures nearby. Here's a guide to some of the best destinations to visit beyond Grenoble, each providing its unique experiences and attractions.

Chartreuse Mountains

The Chartreuse Mountains, located just northeast of Grenoble, are known for their stunning natural beauty and outdoor activities. The region offers a serene escape into nature, with opportunities for hiking, climbing, and exploring charming villages.

La Grande Chartreuse Monastery

The Grande Chartreuse Monastery is the headquarters of the Carthusian order and is nestled deep within the Chartreuse Mountains. While the monastery itself is not open to the public, visitors can explore the museum and visitor center in the nearby village of Saint-Pierre-de-Chartreuse. The museum provides insight into the history of the Carthusian monks and the life at the monastery.

- Address: 38580 Saint-Pierre-de-Chartreuse
- Website: [Musée de la Grande Chartreuse](https://www.grande-chartreuse.fr)

Hiking Trails

The Chartreuse Mountains offer numerous hiking trails, ranging from easy walks to challenging climbs. Popular trails include the Chamechaude Peak, which provides panoramic views of the Alps, and the Pas de l'Ours, known for its scenic beauty and diverse flora.

- Trail Recommendation: Chamechaude Peak Trail
- Difficulty: Moderate to challenging
- Duration: Approximately 4-5 hours round trip

Villages and Local Cuisine

The charming villages of the Chartreuse region, such as Saint-Hilaire-du-Touvet and Saint-Pierre-de-Chartreuse, offer a taste of local life. Enjoy traditional Alpine cuisine at local restaurants, including dishes such as Chartreuse cheese and hearty mountain fare.

- Restaurant Recommendation: Le Refuge du Furon
- Address: 106 Route du Furon, 38660 Saint-Hilaire-du-Touvet
- Website: [Le Refuge du Furon](https://www.refuge-du-furon.com)

Vercors Regional Natural Park

Vercors Regional Natural Park, located southwest of Grenoble, is a diverse natural area known for its rugged landscapes and rich biodiversity. The park is a haven for outdoor enthusiasts and offers various activities throughout the year.

Gorges de la Bourne

The Gorges de la Bourne are spectacular limestone gorges carved by the Bourne River. A scenic drive through the gorges provides breathtaking views, and there are several viewpoints along the route where visitors can stop and take in the natural beauty.

- Address: 38650 Villard-de-Lans
- Website: [Gorges de la Bourne](https://www.parc-du-vercors.fr)

Villard-de-Lans

Villard-de-Lans is a charming alpine town and a popular gateway to the Vercors Park. It offers a range of outdoor activities, including skiing in winter and mountain biking in summer. The town also has a selection of restaurants and shops to explore.

- Restaurant Recommendation: Le Restaurant du Plateau
- Address: 27 Avenue du Professeur Lépine, 38250 Villard-de-Lans
- Website: [Le Restaurant du Plateau](https://www.restaurant-plateau.com)

Caving and Climbing

The Vercors Park is renowned for its caving and climbing opportunities. The park's extensive cave systems, such as the

Grotte de la Luire, provide a unique underground adventure, while the dramatic cliffs offer excellent climbing routes.

- Caving Recommendation: Grotte de la Luire
- Location: Near Pont-en-Royans
- Tours: Available through local adventure companies

Lyon

Lyon, located about 150 kilometers northwest of Grenoble, is France's third-largest city and a UNESCO World Heritage Site. Known for its rich history, vibrant culture, and exceptional cuisine, Lyon is a must-visit destination.

Vieux Lyon

The historic district of Vieux Lyon is characterized by its Renaissance architecture and narrow, cobblestone streets. Explore the traboules (hidden passageways) and visit landmarks such as the Lyon Cathedral and the Basilica of Notre-Dame de Fourvière.

- Address: Vieux Lyon, 69005 Lyon
- Website: [Vieux Lyon](https://www.lyon.fr)

Lyon's Culinary Scene

Lyon is renowned for its culinary heritage, with numerous bouchons (traditional Lyonnais restaurants) serving regional specialties. Try dishes like quenelles (fish dumplings), Lyonnaise salad, and local cheeses.

- Restaurant Recommendation: Le Bouchon des Filles
- Address: 20 Rue des Fantasques, 69001 Lyon
- Website: [Le Bouchon des Filles](https://www.bouchon-des-filles.com)

Annecy

Annecy, often called the "Venice of the Alps," is located about 100 kilometers northeast of Grenoble. The city is famous for its picturesque canals, historic architecture, and stunning lake views.

Lake Annecy

Lake Annecy is one of the cleanest lakes in Europe and offers opportunities for boating, swimming, and scenic walks along the lake's shores. The lakeside promenade is perfect for a leisurely stroll, and boat tours provide a different perspective of the surrounding landscape.

- Address: Lake Annecy, 74000 Annecy
- Website: [Lake Annecy](https://www.lake-annecy.com)

Annecy's Old Town

Annecy's Old Town is a charming area with colorful houses, winding streets, and historic landmarks. Explore the Palais de l'Isle, a medieval castle turned prison, and the Saint-Pierre Cathedral.

- Address: Old Town, 74000 Annecy

- Website: [Annecy's Old Town](https://www.annecy.fr)

Chambéry

Chambéry, located about 120 kilometers east of Grenoble, is a historic city with a rich heritage and beautiful architecture. It serves as a gateway to the Savoie region and offers a range of cultural and historical attractions.

Château de Chambéry

The Château de Chambéry is a historic castle that once served as the residence of the Dukes of Savoy. The castle features an impressive façade, grand halls, and a beautiful courtyard.

- Address: Place du Château, 73000 Chambéry
- Website: [Château de Chambéry](https://www.chateau-chambery.fr)

Chambéry's Old Town

Chambéry's Old Town is a delightful area to explore, with its medieval buildings, quaint streets, and local shops. Don't miss the Fontaine des Éléphants, a notable landmark featuring a fountain with four elephants.

- Address: Old Town, 73000 Chambéry
- Website: [Chambéry's Old Town](https://www.chambery.fr)

Grenoble's location makes it an excellent starting point for exploring a variety of destinations in the French Alps and beyond. Whether you're venturing into the stunning Chartreuse Mountains, discovering the natural beauty of Vercors, enjoying the vibrant city life in Lyon, experiencing the charm of Annecy, or exploring the historic streets of Chambéry, there are plenty of opportunities for memorable day trips and excursions. Each destination offers its unique attractions and experiences, ensuring that your time in the region is as enriching as it is enjoyable.

Chapter 13 Fun for All Ages

Grenoble is a fantastic destination for families, offering a variety of activities and attractions that cater to all ages. From engaging museums to expansive parks and interactive exhibits, there's something to keep children and adults entertained. Here's a guide to some of the best family-friendly activities in and around Grenoble.

Family-Friendly Museums

Museums in Grenoble offer a range of educational and entertaining experiences for families. These institutions provide interactive exhibits and hands-on activities that make learning fun for children and adults alike.

Grenoble Museum

The Grenoble Museum (Musée de Grenoble) is known for its extensive collection of fine arts, including works from the Renaissance to contemporary pieces. The museum frequently organizes family-oriented workshops and interactive tours that make art accessible and engaging for children.

- Address: 5 Place de Lavalette, 38000 Grenoble
- Website: [Grenoble Museum](https://www.museedegrenoble.fr)

Musée Dauphinois

The Musée Dauphinois explores the cultural and natural heritage of the Dauphiné region through a variety of exhibits. The museum's interactive displays and workshops are designed to engage children and provide insights into local history and traditions.

- Address: 30 Rue Maurice-Gignoux, 38000 Grenoble
- Website: [Musée Dauphinois](https://www.museedauphinois.fr)

La Casemate

La Casemate is a science and technology museum that focuses on making science accessible and exciting for all ages. With interactive exhibits, hands-on experiments, and a dedicated children's area, it's an excellent place for family visits.

- Address: 4 Rue de la République, 38000 Grenoble
- Website: [La Casemate](https://www.lacasemate.fr)

Parks and Playgrounds

Grenoble's parks and playgrounds offer plenty of space for children to play and families to relax. These green spaces provide a break from sightseeing and a chance to enjoy the outdoors.

Paul Mistral Park

Paul Mistral Park is a large, central park in Grenoble that features wide open spaces, playgrounds, and sports facilities. The park's playgrounds are well-equipped with modern play structures, and the vast lawns provide plenty of room for picnics and outdoor games.

- Address: 29 Avenue du Doyen Gosse, 38000 Grenoble
- Website: [Paul Mistral Park](https://www.grenoble.fr)

Jardin de Ville

Jardin de Ville is a beautifully landscaped park with a large playground that is perfect for younger children. The park features shaded areas, walking paths, and a pond, making it a peaceful retreat in the heart of the city.

- Address: 1 Place du Général de Gaulle, 38000 Grenoble
- Website: [Jardin de Ville](https://www.grenoble.fr)

Parc de la Poya

Parc de la Poya is a family-friendly park with a range of amenities, including a large playground, sports fields, and picnic areas. The park's natural setting provides a great environment for outdoor activities and family gatherings.

- Address: 12 Rue des Flandres-Dunkerque, 38100 Grenoble
- Website: [Parc de la Poya](https://www.grenoble.fr)

Interactive Exhibits

Interactive exhibits and activities can make learning fun for kids, providing hands-on experiences that stimulate curiosity and creativity.

Le Magasin – Centre National d'Art Contemporain

Le Magasin, while primarily an art center, occasionally hosts interactive exhibits and workshops designed for families and children. These activities encourage creativity and provide a unique way to engage with contemporary art.

- Address: 8 Esplanade Andry-Farcy, 38000 Grenoble
- Website: [Le Magasin](https://www.magasin-cnac.org)

The Natural History Museum of Grenoble

The Natural History Museum offers interactive exhibits and educational displays that explore the natural world. With sections dedicated to geology, paleontology, and biology, the museum provides a fascinating and educational experience for children.

- Address: 1 Rue Dolomieu, 38000 Grenoble
- Website: [Natural History Museum of Grenoble](https://www.museum-grenoble.fr)

Kid-Friendly Restaurants

Dining out with kids can be a challenge, but Grenoble offers several restaurants that cater to families with children, providing menus and environments suited to younger diners.

La Table de l'Ours

La Table de l'Ours is a family-friendly restaurant known for its welcoming atmosphere and varied menu. The restaurant offers a selection of dishes that appeal to both adults and children, including kid-friendly options and high chairs.

- Address: 16 Rue de Strasbourg, 38000 Grenoble
- Website: [La Table de l'Ours](https://www.latabledelours.com)

Le Café des Arts

Le Café des Arts offers a relaxed dining experience with a menu that includes options for children. The restaurant's casual atmosphere and friendly staff make it a great choice for families.

- Address: 24 Rue Paul Claudel, 38100 Grenoble
- Website: [Le Café des Arts](https://www.cafedesarts-grenoble.com)

La Crêperie des Alpes

La Crêperie des Alpes specializes in crêpes and galettes, offering a variety of sweet and savory options that are popular with kids. The restaurant's colorful decor and playful menu make it a hit with families.

- Address: 5 Rue de la République, 38000 Grenoble
- Website: [La Crêperie des Alpes](https://www.creperie-alpes.com)

Grenoble is well-equipped to provide a fun and engaging experience for families. From interactive museums and expansive parks to kid-friendly restaurants, the city offers a variety of activities that cater to all ages. These family-friendly options ensure that everyone, from toddlers to teens, can enjoy their time in Grenoble and create lasting memories together.

Chapter 14: Visitor Essentials

When traveling to Grenoble, it's important to be well-prepared with essential information to ensure a smooth and enjoyable visit. Here's a comprehensive guide to help you navigate the practical aspects of your trip, from finding tourist information to understanding local customs.

Tourist Information Centers

Tourist information centers are valuable resources for visitors, providing maps, brochures, and advice on attractions and services.

Grenoble Tourist Office

The Grenoble Tourist Office is located in the city center and offers a wide range of services for tourists. Here you can get information about local attractions, transportation, guided tours, and events happening during your stay.

- Address: 14 Rue Very, 38000 Grenoble
- Hours: Monday to Saturday, 9:00 AM – 6:00 PM; Closed on Sundays
- Website: [Grenoble Tourist Office](https://www.grenoble-tourisme.com)

Grenoble-Alpes Métropole Tourist Office

This office provides information not just for Grenoble but also for the surrounding metropolitan area. It's a good resource for learning about regional attractions and activities.

- Address: 4 Avenue de la Gare, 38000 Grenoble
- Hours: Monday to Friday, 9:00 AM – 5:00 PM
- Website: [Grenoble-Alpes Métropole](https://www.grenoble-alpes-metropole.fr)

Emergency Contacts

Knowing how to contact emergency services and other key contacts can be crucial during your trip.

Emergency Services

- Police: 17
- Ambulance and Fire: 18
- European Emergency Number: 112

Medical Services

Grenoble University Hospital

- Address: 38043 Grenoble
- Phone: +33 4 76 76 76 76
- Website: [Grenoble University Hospital](https://www.chu-grenoble.fr)

Pharmacies: Many pharmacies in Grenoble have extended hours and offer emergency services. Look for signs reading "Pharmacie de Garde" for pharmacies on call.

Local Customs and Etiquette

Understanding local customs and etiquette will enhance your experience and show respect for the local culture.

Greetings and Communication

- Greetings: A common greeting is a handshake. Among friends, a kiss on both cheeks is customary.

It's polite to greet people with "Bonjour" (Good morning) or "Bonsoir" (Good evening).
- Language: While French is the official language, many people in the tourist industry speak English. However, learning a few basic French phrases can be helpful and appreciated.

Dining Etiquette
- Tipping: Service charge is included in the bill in restaurants, but leaving a small tip (5-10%) for good service is appreciated.
- Table Manners: Keep your hands on the table (not your elbows) and use utensils properly. It's customary to wait for everyone to be served before starting your meal.

Currency and Banking

Currency

- **Currency**: The currency used in Grenoble is the Euro (€). ATMs are widely available, and credit and debit cards are commonly accepted in most establishments.

Banking Services
- ATMs: ATMs are easily found throughout Grenoble, especially in the city center and near major shopping areas.

- Banks: Major banks in Grenoble include BNP Paribas, Société Générale, and Crédit Agricole. Banking hours are generally Monday to Friday, 9:00 AM – 5:00 PM.

Currency Exchange

- **Currency Exchange Offices**: These can be found at the train station, in the city center, and at the airport. Rates may vary, so it's advisable to compare a few options.

Language Tips

Basic French Phrases

- Hello/Goodbye: Bonjour / Au revoir
- Please: S'il vous plaît
- Thank you: Merci
- Yes/No: Oui / Non
- Excuse me: Excusez-moi
- Do you speak English?: Parlez-vous anglais?

Pronunciation Tips

- Accent: The French "r" is pronounced from the back of the throat, and vowels can be nasalized.
- Politeness: Always use "vous" when addressing strangers or in formal situations. "Tu" is used for informal settings with people you know well.

Having practical information at your fingertips can significantly enhance your travel experience in Grenoble. From knowing where to get tourist information and emergency contacts to understanding local customs and managing your currency, these essentials will help you navigate the city with ease. By familiarizing yourself with these aspects before your trip, you can focus on enjoying all that Grenoble has to offer.

Chapter 15: Making the Most of Your Visit

Grenoble is a vibrant city with a lot to offer, and with some preparation, you can make the most of your trip. Here's a guide to help you plan your visit effectively, from choosing the best time to go to practicing eco-friendly travel.

Best Times to Visit

Grenoble offers unique experiences throughout the year, each season providing its own charm.

Spring (March to May)

Spring is an ideal time to visit Grenoble, with mild weather and blooming flowers making outdoor activities especially enjoyable. Temperatures range from 10°C to 20°C (50°F to

68°F), perfect for exploring parks, hiking trails, and enjoying the city's outdoor cafés.

Summer (June to August)

Summer in Grenoble can be warm, with temperatures averaging between 20°C and 30°C (68°F to 86°F). It's a great time for outdoor activities such as hiking and mountain biking. The summer months also bring various festivals and events, adding to the city's lively atmosphere. However, be prepared for crowds and higher accommodation prices.

Autumn (September to November)

Autumn offers cooler temperatures and stunning fall foliage, making it a picturesque time to visit. Temperatures range from 10°C to 20°C (50°F to 68°F). This season is ideal for hiking and exploring the surrounding mountains as the weather remains pleasant and the tourist crowds thin out.

Winter (December to February)

Winter in Grenoble is cold, with temperatures ranging from -5°C to 5°C (23°F to 41°F). This season is perfect for skiing and snowboarding in the nearby Alps. While the weather can be chilly, the snowy landscape creates a beautiful setting for winter sports and festive activities.

Safety Tips

Grenoble is generally a safe city for tourists, but it's always wise to stay informed and cautious.

General Safety

- Personal Belongings: Keep an eye on your belongings, especially in crowded areas or public transport. Use a money belt or a secure bag for valuables.
- Emergency Contacts: Familiarize yourself with emergency services and know the local emergency numbers.
- Health Precautions: In case of health issues, make sure to have travel insurance that covers medical expenses. The city has good healthcare facilities and pharmacies.

Travel Safety

- Transportation: Use reputable transportation services. If using taxis, prefer official taxis and ensure the meter is running.
- Safe Areas: Stick to well-lit and populated areas at night. The city center and popular neighborhoods are generally safe, but it's always good to stay alert.

Budgeting for Your Trip

Grenoble offers a range of options for different budgets, from luxury accommodations to budget-friendly choices.

Accommodation Costs

- Luxury Hotels: Prices can range from €150 to €300 per night.

- Mid-Range Hotels: Expect to pay between €70 and €150 per night.
- Budget Hotels and Hostels: Rates can be as low as €30 to €70 per night.

Dining Costs

- Restaurants: A meal at a mid-range restaurant may cost around €20 to €40 per person. Budget restaurants and cafés offer meals for around €10 to €15.
- Groceries: Shopping for groceries can help reduce costs. A budget of €40 to €60 per week for groceries should suffice for a moderate eater.

Transportation Costs

- Public Transport: A single ticket for buses or trams costs around €1.50. Consider purchasing a multi-day pass if you plan to use public transport frequently.
- Car Rentals: Prices vary based on the car type and rental duration but typically start around €30 to €50 per day.

Eco-Friendly Travel Practices

Grenoble is committed to sustainability, and there are several ways you can travel more responsibly during your visit.

Sustainable Transportation

- Public Transport: Use the city's excellent public transport system to reduce your carbon footprint. Trams, buses, and bikes are eco-friendly options.
- Cycling: Grenoble is a bike-friendly city with dedicated cycling paths. Renting a bicycle is a great way to explore the city while minimizing your environmental impact.

Responsible Tourism

- Reduce Waste: Carry a reusable water bottle and shopping bags to reduce plastic waste. Many places offer refill stations for water.
- Support Local Businesses: Choose local shops, restaurants, and markets to support the local economy and reduce the carbon footprint associated with imported goods.

Conservation Efforts

- Respect Nature: When exploring natural areas, follow designated trails and respect wildlife. Avoid littering and adhere to park regulations.
- Energy and Water Use: Be mindful of energy and water use in accommodations. Turn off lights and appliances when not in use, and conserve water.

With careful planning and consideration, your visit to Grenoble can be both enjoyable and responsible. By choosing the right time to visit, staying safe, budgeting effectively, and practicing eco-friendly travel habits, you can make the most of your trip and contribute positively to the city's environment and community. Whether you're exploring the city's cultural sites, enjoying outdoor adventures, or simply relaxing in a café, Grenoble offers a memorable experience for every traveler.

Chapter 16: Grenoble for Business

Grenoble is not only a picturesque destination but also a vibrant hub for business and innovation. With its cutting-edge facilities, diverse networking opportunities, and supportive business environment, the city is well-equipped to cater to professionals and business travelers. Here's a detailed guide to navigating Grenoble for business purposes.

Conference Venues

Grenoble boasts a range of modern and versatile conference venues suitable for events of all sizes.

WTC Grenoble (World Trade Center Grenoble)

The WTC Grenoble is a premier venue for conferences, seminars, and corporate events. Located in the heart of the city, it offers state-of-the-art facilities, including meeting rooms, exhibition spaces, and a large auditorium.

- Address: 1 Place Robert Schuman, 38000 Grenoble
- Capacity: Up to 1,000 participants
- Website: [WTC Grenoble](https://www.wtc-grenoble.com)

Palais des Congrès de Grenoble

This well-known conference center provides a range of facilities for international conferences, exhibitions, and conventions. The Palais des Congrès is equipped with modern technology and offers flexible room configurations.

- Address: 5-7 Place Robert Schuman, 38000 Grenoble
- Capacity: Up to 2,500 participants
- Website: [Palais des Congrès](https://www.palaisdescongres-grenoble.com)

La Caserne de Bonne

La Caserne de Bonne is a unique venue that combines historical charm with contemporary facilities. It's ideal for corporate events and meetings, offering a variety of spaces in a distinctive setting.

- Address: 3 Rue de la Caserne de Bonne, 38000 Grenoble
- Capacity: Various rooms accommodating up to 500 participants

- Website: [La Caserne de Bonne](https://www.caserne-de-bonne.com)

Business Services

Grenoble provides a comprehensive range of business services to support your professional needs.

Co-Working Spaces

Coworking Grenoble: Located centrally, Coworking Grenoble offers flexible workspaces, meeting rooms, and high-speed internet. It's a great spot for freelancers and business travelers needing a productive environment.

- Address: 7 Rue de l'Industrie, 38000 Grenoble
- Website: [Coworking Grenoble](https://www.coworking-grenoble.com)

La Cordée: This co-working space emphasizes community and collaboration, providing not only workspace but also networking events and workshops.

- Address: 2 Rue Félix Viallet, 38000 Grenoble
- Website: [La Cordée](https://www.lacordee.net)

Business Centers

Regus Grenoble: Regus offers fully serviced office spaces and meeting rooms in various locations around the city, ideal for temporary needs and business meetings.

- Address: 4 Avenue Maréchal Foch, 38000 Grenoble
- Website: [Regus Grenoble](https://www.regus.com)

Buro Club Grenoble: This business center provides flexible office solutions, virtual offices, and meeting rooms with modern amenities.

- Address: 5 Rue de la Liberté, 38000 Grenoble
- Website: [Buro Club Grenoble](https://www.buro.com)

Networking Spots

Grenoble has numerous venues and events where business professionals can network and build connections.

Business Lunch Spots

Le Bistrot du Palais: This restaurant offers a relaxed atmosphere ideal for business lunches. It serves traditional French cuisine and is popular with local professionals.

- Address: 11 Place Grenette, 38000 Grenoble
- Website: [Le Bistrot du Palais](https://www.bistrotdupalais.com)

Brasserie du Théâtre: Located near the city's cultural district, this brasserie combines excellent cuisine with a sophisticated setting, making it a great choice for business meals.

- Address: 12 Rue Pierre-Sémard, 38000 Grenoble
- Website: [Brasserie du Théâtre](https://www.brasseriedutheatre.com)

Networking Events and Conferences

Grenoble Alpes Start-Up: This organization hosts various networking events and conferences focused on entrepreneurship and innovation in the region.

- Website: [Grenoble Alpes Start-Up](https://www.grenoble-alpes-startup.fr)

Grenoble Business Club: Regular meetings and events organized by this club offer opportunities to connect with local business leaders and professionals.

- Website: [Grenoble Business Club](https://www.grenoble-business-club.fr)

Tips for Business Travelers

To ensure a productive and smooth business trip to Grenoble, consider these practical tips:

Communication

- Language: While many professionals in Grenoble speak English, learning a few French phrases can be beneficial and is often appreciated in a business setting.

- Email and Phone: Ensure your email and phone are set up for international communication. Local SIM cards or international plans can help manage costs.

Time Management

- Schedule: Plan your meetings and appointments well in advance. Grenoble's public transport system is reliable, but allow extra time for travel between appointments.
- Local Time: Grenoble is in the Central European Time (CET) zone, so adjust your schedule accordingly if you're traveling from a different time zone.

Local Etiquette

- Professionalism: Punctuality is valued in the business culture. Arriving on time for meetings and events reflects well on you.
- Business Cards: Exchange business cards with both hands and take a moment to review the card you receive, showing respect for the contact's position.

Accommodation

- Proximity: Choose accommodations close to your business meetings or events to minimize travel time and maximize productivity.

- Amenities: Opt for hotels that offer business services such as meeting rooms, high-speed internet, and printing facilities.

Grenoble offers a robust environment for business travelers, with excellent conference venues, comprehensive business services, and ample networking opportunities. By leveraging these resources and adhering to local customs, you can ensure a successful and enjoyable business trip. Whether you're attending a major conference, meeting clients, or exploring opportunities in this dynamic city, Grenoble provides a supportive and sophisticated backdrop for your professional endeavors.

Printed in Great Britain
by Amazon